HOW TO LAND AN EXCELLENT BUSINESS INTERNSHIP

By Michael P. Griffin

Charlton College of Business, University of Massachusetts Dartmouth

North Dartmouth, Massachusetts

Swansea Publishing Group

Swansea, Massachusetts

© 2012 Michael P. Griffin

Published by Swansea Publishing Group
808 Wood Street
Swansea, Massachusetts
ISBN: 978-1-105-89465-7

All rights reserved. The text of this publication or any part thereof, may not be reproduced in any manner whatsoever without the written permission from the publisher.

Bulk orders available upon request. Digital versions of book are also available. Email: mgriffin@umassd.edu

How to Land an Excellent Business Internship

INTERNSHIP PROGRAMS at colleges are run by administrators–deans, department chairs, internship directors and career planning coordinators. As the internship director, I am one of those administrators, therefore, when students at our business college want an internship they get in touch with me. The question I often get from these students is: "Can you find me an internship?" My answer is usually something like: "No–but I can tell you how you can go about starting a process that may lead you to landing an internship." I cannot place students into internships. There just aren't enough internship opportunities to go around and to find a suitable one takes some time and effort. My advice to students looking for an excellent internship is to learn and work the process and the odds of finding one will increase dramatically. That's what this book is about.

Researching and identifying an internship that might be suitable for a particular student is a process and usually requires more time and preparation than most students realize. You must remain patient and positive; great leads may come at any time and from a variety of sources. Knowing what sources to tap into is half the battle and that is the purpose of this special book: learning how to utilize various sources of internship leads.

The tips and strategies that I mention in this booklet are all proven. In my years as internship director at the Charlton College of Business I have collected information from the hundreds of undergraduates who have earned credits by completing internships. Some of the information that I have gathered from our students provides the details of how to land an excellent internship--the toughest task of all in our program.

In watching how our students land an internship, I have concluded that there is no one proven or best way. Many approaches need to be executed and I have included details within this book of successful strategies that I have seen over the years.

When talking to students about how to find a great internship, I can't help but think of one of my favorite cartoons I watched as a small child–"Felix the Cat"[1] . Felix was a feline who would get in a lot of trouble, but he could extricate himself from just about any jam by

---

[1] "Felix the Cat" was originally the title of a a comic strip but was made into 260 television cartoons distributed by Trans-Lux beginning in 1958. In 2002, Felix was voted in TV Guide's 50 greatest cartoon characters of all time, ranking #28.

reaching into his "bag of tricks"—a magical satchel that Felix always carried with him. Students need to develop a bag of tricks when they are looking for internships (and jobs). No one approach is enough to generate an adequate number of quality internship leads. And like the sales and marketing function of a business, good opportunities will come only when you generate some solid leads. Generating those leads will take imagination, persistence, networking, and research.

Use Your Imagination and Connect with Professionals

IMAGINE THE VARIOUS POSSIBILITIES from which an internship lead may come. Find ways to be in touch and connected to potential employers. Be creative and take advantage of any opportunities that give you the chance to communicate with a potential internship provider. Although I post many internship opportunities on our college blog, I encourage students to search on their own and to explore what is out there and to come back to me with proposals. One thing that all business students should know is that many employers are looking for interns, and many others could be easily convinced that an internship is a good idea.

You can make your own luck with landing an internship by being aggressive in your search. In our region there is a beer maker by the name of Narragansett (www.narragansettbeer.com). A product of nearby Rhode Island, Narragansett Beer was very popular during the 1950s and 60s and was a sponsor of Boston Red Sox games on television. I can still hear the advertising slogan, "Hi, Neighbor, have a 'Gansett!," most famously uttered by Boston Red Sox announcer Curt Gowdy. During the later part of the 20th century, Narragansett fell on tough times and the Rhode Island brewery was closed. The brand was eventually acquired in 2005 by a team of local Rhode Island investors led by the former CEO of Nantucket Nectars, Mark D. Hellendrung. I noticed that Mr. Hellendrung was giving a talk at one of our business events and ironically, a student contacted me about an internship with Narragansett.

I suggested that the student show up at Mr. Hellendrung's talk and the young man did just that. He listened to Hellendrung's discussion, asked great questions, and after the presentation approached Mr. Hellendrung with a business card and a request for an internship. The student eventually landed the internship with Narragansett and it was an excellent experience. That type of networking can land a student a dream internship.

If you want to maximize your chances of landing a great internship, do not wait for an opportunity to show up on your college's website. A great number of successful internships happen because students find them by their own means. Sometimes we (college administrators) have almost nothing to do with students landing the perfect internships. Many times these are the best situations in part because the student digs to uncover them, causing the student to develop a real sense of ownership with the internship. Again, the point is that there are many approaches to landing an excellent internship. I have had students work with our career resource center to find a good opportunity or send résumés to area companies. I have also had students uncover great opportunities by leaving their résumés and our internship brochure with business back in their hometowns.

Sometimes setting up an internship means getting out into the real world and hustling to make things happen–to generate good internship leads. One student, Jessica, landed an excellent fall semester accounting internship with a regional CPA firm that was about 30 miles from our campus. She was the first student from our school to successfully complete an internship with that firm and by Thanksgiving of her senior year, was assured a well paying full-time job with that firm.

That's a success story that I always recall when students ask me how to uncover good opportunities. Jessica achieved this all by going outside of her comfort zone and taking the initiative to find her own career transforming internship. I was extremely pleased to learn that after a couple of years on the job, Jessica had passed the CPA exam and was well established in her public accounting career.

If you are interested in landing a great internship you will need to hustle and do some research. Internships are competitive situations and you need to do whatever you can to give yourself an edge. The opportunity probably won't be handed to you. Professors, deans, internship directors and others at your school can sometimes advocate for you or recommend you to an employer for an internship position. However, do not count on that. You need to be proactive, prepared, and eager.

Career Planning Office, Faculty, and Student Peers

IT IS TRUE THAT LOCAL EMPLOYERS and sometimes national firms contact university career planning offices, business deans, department chairs, and faculty with requests for interns. Area employers contact our college with internship opportunities almost weekly. In turn, these opportunities are promoted to business students via email, website postings, and word of mouth. Faculty make announcements in class and our student advisors point students in the right direction. Therefore, by a variety of communications, interested students are informed about the various internship opportunities, but the number of internship opportunities that show up at the doorstep of a college or university is never enough to meet the demand, in fact, it is not even close. For example, our program grants credit to about 100 internships each year, but that is only the tip of the iceberg when it comes to potential demand. Our junior and senior business majors are eligible to do an internship for credit and there are about 800 of them.

Some schools such as the world famous Fuqua School of business at Duke University solicit the assistance of students who have already gone through the internship search. Each year the career management center at Duke selects sixty or so students that are career fellows—second-year students that have already been through the job-search process and have had successful summer internships. They work with the first-year students, by industry and functional area, on résumés, cover letters, and mock interviews.

Peers helping interested students find solid internships are one possibility, which Duke has mastered in a very formal process. Less formal processes of peer help can come about by active involvement in college clubs and associations. If your school has an approach similar to the Duke peer support, take advantage of it.

If your school has an internship director, meet with him or her to find out how internship announcements are made. Are they blasted out via email, posted on a blog, entered into a software system, or set up on the web? If your college has a career resource center, visit the center and find out how they can help you land a good internship. There are people at your school that have a passion for internships. Identify who they are and begin to work with them to uncover great opportunities, but also keep in mind that the most you can hope for is guidance. You will need to do the majority of the work. You need to be the person making the contacts, handing out the business cards, and sending the résumés.

Think about the type of internship that will help you meet your personal goals. Think about your reasons for wanting an internship. Make a list of your interests, skills, career aspirations, and exactly what you want to accomplish in the 15 weeks or so that you will be interning.

For example, an internship with a local CPA firm or a summer internship with one of the national firms makes sense for an accounting student planning on a career in public accounting. However, if an accounting major wants to go into management accounting, an internship as a staff accountant or internal auditor might make more sense. The point is that before you target certain potential internship providers, know thyself.

Know What You Want

KNOW WHAT YOU WANT IN AN internship. Ask yourself some more questions:

- What do I want to get out of an internship?
- Do I want to do an internship during the summer or the fall or spring semesters?
- Can I afford an unpaid internship?

It may be that your search for an internship will have constraints. There may be a particular semester that makes the most sense or it might be that you need to be paid to keep afloat.

Constraints are part of life. Identify your constraining factors and focus your search appropriately. If you give yourself enough time, utilize the right resources, and work hard enough, you will find and opportunity that will match up well with what you want to accomplish.

At our business college, we have many students who do an internship in the summer, but such an internship, if the student wants to earn credit, comes with a constraint. Students must pay for a summer internship cost and the tuition is more than $1,000. For many students that means, unless they get financial assistance, that they must find a paid internship so they can afford the internship class.

Working Your Search

I CAN'T EMPHASIZE ENOUGH THE NEED to be proactive in your search. Don't wait for someone to find you an internship. One of the valuable aspects of an internship is that you call some of the shots. You have a chance to be proactive and shape your learning experience right from the start. Explore possibilities on your own.

I tell students to review job listings in the Sunday classified ads of our local papers: the Boston Globe, Providence Journal, New Bedford Standard Times, and the Fall River Herald News.

Although companies rarely advertise internships in the newspaper, you may discover a contact person to whom you can send your own cover letter and résumé inquiring or proposing an internship. Once again, I can't over emphasize how developing "leads" is a key to landing your own internship.

Consider sending a letter of inquiry and your résumé to any prospective employers that you think could offer you a great internship experience. Think about the products and services that you value and who produces them. Do they have operations within commuting distances of your home or school? Are there any nonprofits in the area that are well run or provide their stakeholders with services that you have seen as critical or making a difference? What government agencies are in your area that you could intern at?

An example inquiry (cover) letter is contained towards the end of this chapter. Tailor it to meet your specific needs and send out 10–20 to test the market. Finding a great internship is a trial-and-error process. You need to take some risks and the risk with a test mailing is that you will spend the money on postage and stationary and not even get an interview. That is a chance you must be willing to take if you want to explore all sources.

Search online job banks for internships. Perhaps your career resource center can help you learn how to do this. Services such as "Indeed.com" and "Simply Hired" are useful portals for students looking for the first job or an internship. Since online services are updated each day, you need to visit frequently and respond quickly to any internship opportunities that interest you.

Keep in mind that just like finding your first job, an internship opportunity may not come from an online site. You have to utilize all sources, including career fairs and other networking opportunities.

Attend a career fair (on campus or off campus) and discuss your desire to land a great internship with recruiters. Some employers will be only interested in students who can work full-time or who are on the verge of graduating. However, some employers will recognize talent when they see it and be open to developing an internship. Keep in mind that companies that participate in job fairs are trying to recruit talent and an internship is definitely a recruiting tool, and a low risk one at that. Follow-up any potential leads that you cultivate at a job fair with a résumé and cover letter.

Let your business professors, your parents, and your parents' colleagues, friends, and neighbors know that you are looking for an internship. They may know people in the industry who are looking for an intern. Accounting professors know practitioners, operations management faculty know people who run factories, and marketing professors know people who run advertising agencies. These are valuable contacts and part of a faculty member's job should be to connect students with the business community.

By getting the word out to your network of contacts, which includes your parents and any working adult that you know, you increase your odds of finding the right internship. Many business professors have contacts with businesses and nonprofits and your parents and other working adults have networks of contacts that can come up with internships. I once saw a statistic that 15–20% of all available jobs are not advertised. I suspect that the same statistic for internships is probably higher. That's why networking is critical to your success.

Student Peers as a Source of Internship Leads

TALK TO OTHER STUDENTS WHO HAVE completed internships. Your peers are a great source of information regarding internships. They can give you firsthand knowledge about the employer and whether they think the experience was worth the time and effort. Networking through fellow students, parents, and friends can be the best way to land a great internship. This is a powerful internship network at our college.

Students who complete successful internships tell their friends. I receive countless emails and phone calls from students who tell me their friend completed an internship at XYZ Corporation and recommended the experience. I suggest you should post to Facebook and tweet your friends that you are looking for internship leads.

Have Business Cards Made

HAVE BUSINESS CARDS MADE that you can hand out to people that you meet. A business card is relatively small and you can easily bring it anywhere. Despite all the publicity about social networks such as Facebook and LinkedIn, and how connecting with people is effective through the virtual world, the old fashion practice of giving out a business card is still an effective means of making a contact. Companies like Vista Print (www.vistaprint.com) Moo.com, and Staples Office Supply stores periodically offer free business cards. Vista Print typically gives away 250 copies of a basic business card as a way of introducing customers to its online services. The cards at MOO.com are very creative and colorful.

Some of the styles of MOO.com cards might be a bit to creative for some prospective employers so my advice is if you use MOO.com, stay conservative with color and style when you design your cards. However, for some of the creative internship possibilities–like marketing, web design, etc., the MOO.com cards may be a great fit.

Handing a business card to a new person that you meet is a gesture that initiates a step towards building relationships. The business card will help your new contact remember your name, give them your contact information, and provide a source document for their database of contacts. A business card and a well-done résumé is an absolute must for your bag of tricks. Remember Felix the Cat!

Subscribe to email Alerts

SUBSCRIBE TO AN EMAIL ALERT SERVICE that can tell you when an internship posting has been made on the web. I subscribe to one through a website called Indeed.com (www.indeed.com) and it has been quite fruitful. Another service that we have had good luck with is Simply Hired (www.simplyhired.com). These services send me an email once a day based on the keywords that I enter. For example, I receive an email alert for any web job posting that includes the words: "Internships in Massachusetts." As a result, I have been able to alert our business students to internship openings with companies such as State Street Bank, Proctor and Gamble, the New England Patriots, Nike, Reebok, and PricewaterhouseCoopers, just to name a few. Students who respond quickly to these email alerts have had good luck landing internships.

Learn how to do advance searching with these sites. For example, with Simply Hired you can incorporate filters such as:

- Keywords found anywhere in a job posting

- Keywords found in job titles

- Locations based on a certain number of miles (radius) from a particular city (5, 10, 15, 25, 50, and 100 miles)

- Freshness of the posting such as postings since your last visit to the site, last 24 hours, last 7 days, last 30 days etc.

- Company size (based on number of employees and/or revenues)

Some students have difficulty mastering setting up effective searches that yield good results. At many colleges, personnel in the career resource center or a business librarian can teach how to set up an effective search for internships that will yield good results and those results along with daily email alerts can provide a good set of leads.

Most internship postings online require that you apply through the company's job portal. Some require that you build an online profile and some job portals will allow you to import an existing profile from a social networking site such as LinkedIn. Therefore, it makes sense to have a LinkedIn profile already in place as it provides recruiters with the latest information regarding your education and work history, making it easy to keep a profile on a job portal constantly up-to-date.

Prepare Your Own Mailing List

IF YOU ARE INTERESTED IN FINDING your own internship, one strategy you can try is to send a letter of inquiry and your résumé to companies and organizations in the region. Finding a mailing list of companies is the key. You can use the yellow pages, but be careful to identify organizations that are likely to offer internships. You want to be sure that the company you identify has the type of operation and professional environment that you are seeking. Some locations only have small sales offices or some other phase of the value chain in which you are not interested.

Some business oriented newspapers offer a book of lists. Check to see if there is such a list in your region. You may want to consult with the reference librarian. For example, our business librarian alerted me to the fact that in our region there is a newspaper called the "Providence Business News" (PBN). Providence, RI is the largest metropolitan area within a thirty-mile radius of our university. Annually, "PBN" publishes its "Book of Lists." These lists include the largest organizations in the region in such categories as Accounting Firms, Advertising Agencies, Banks, Hospitals, Manufacturers, and Insurance companies.

By perusing that publication, students may come upon a company that is of interest to them or perhaps they may have friends or family members who work for one of the companies and may be able to connect them an internship sponsor.

I have also suggested that students look at lists of the largest employers within a fifty-mile radius of our campus. That type of information can be found on the web or perhaps obtained from local chambers of commerce and in some cases, from the Career Resource Center of your school. Our internship program is operated out of our college of business but in some schools, the Career Resource Center takes a more active role in identifying possible internship providers and your career development office might be able to provide you with a list of internship companies. In addition, many colleges and universities are successful in connecting alumni with current students for internship match-making. Your school's alumni office might have ideas on how you can make such a connection.

For accounting majors interested in doing an internship at a CPA firm, many of the state societies of CPAs publish a guide or web-based resource that lists member firms and contact names, websites, street addresses, and email addresses. In Massachusetts our society of CPAs (www.mscpaonline.org) publishes a very useful guide called the College Guide. It lists profiles all the CPA firms in Massachusetts, including email addresses.

Tap into Alumni

DUKE UNIVERSITY HAS A SERVICE called DukeConnect. which allows students who are interested in doing an internship to connect with Duke Alumni in the same field. Duke undergrads are able to locate Duke alumni who are willing to hire them as interns and mentor them through the process. My experience with alumni from our business school is that many are eager to share their knowledge and to help students land internships and in some cases, permanent jobs. DukeConnect is an awesome database of over 5,000 professionals. Your college may not have such a service although more and more schools are building such databases to help with the search for jobs and internships.

If your school doesn't have a formal alumni connect system keep in mind that connecting with alumni is still possible. Watch for alumni events that you can participate in. Many student associations and clubs invite alumni to participate as speakers or panel members. Attend those events and introduce yourself to as many professionals as possible.

One of the great things about an internship provider who is also an alumnus of your college is that they will be a great advocate for you within the organization. This will help increase the chances that your internship experience will be an excellent one. In addition, alumni guided internships are usually reoccurring. For example, we are fortunate to have several accounting and finance alumni working at the international conglomerate known as Textron. Textron's headquarters are located in Providence, RI–about 1/2 commute from our campus. Each year, Textron executives get in touch with me and request an intern; a sustainable flow of opportunities. This same situation is also happening with local banks, CPA firms, and one well known manufacturer. I am always so confident that these internships will always work out to be the best work experiences for our students because we have our alumni looking out for the next wave of business students and new graduates.

Think about how you can tap into the alumni of your school. What's the most valuable outcome of your college years? If you think it's your degree or the learning that you accomplished, you're only partially right. Beyond the degrees or the knowledge you are gaining in college, your alumni network will someday be one of the most important benefits of your college years. Alumni are experienced professionals, industry experts, potential clients and trusted colleagues---in short; they are people who can help you land a great internship. Social networking sites, like LinkedIn may help you connect with alumni from your school - folks who can advocate for you within their firm or who may be looking for an intern just like you. For example, if I go into my LinkedIn account and look at my contacts, I can see that from Bryant University, my alma mater, there are almost 19,000 alums living in the United States (as of June 2012) and about 5,000 of them living in the Providence, RI area, the closest city to where I live. I can also filter those alumni by the companies that employ them.

Join Student Clubs and Associations

OVER THE YEARS, many students at my business college have landed business internships after meeting an employer at a student club or association dinner or meeting. For example, at the Charlton College of Business, we have an accounting association. Its purpose is to introduce students to the profession of accounting and to practitioners of accounting. I know several students who have attended such gatherings and have impressed participants from the public accounting world and from management accounting, and as a result, have obtained excellent internships.

Other popular clubs and associations include investment clubs, Students in Free Enterprise (SIFE), NetImpact (a network of emerging business leaders dedicated to using the power of business to create a better world), and the Advertising Association. If you want to find a quality internship, you should probably join some student clubs and get involved! More internships and job offers come from networking sources than from any other source.

In addition to joining student run clubs, many students have found that professional organizations have student memberships at much reduced rates with many of the benefits that full members enjoy. In my area of expertise, accounting, there are student memberships for the Institute of Management Accountants, the American Association of Certified Fraud Examiners, the Institute of Internal Auditors and the state societies of CPAs. In marketing, the American Management Association has a student membership as does the American Management Association. These types of organizations invite student members to their local and regional meetings where students can mingle and meet professionals in their fields of interest. It is quite possible that through this type of networking, you can generate some interesting internship leads.

The Washington Center (TWC)

IF YOU ARE LOOKING FOR AN internship in business or government and want to have your experience in the Washington D.C. area, the

Washington Center should be the first on your list of great internship sources. We have had several students complete Washington Center internships and I have visited internship sites in the DC area and have been very impressed with the program.

There is a sequence of steps necessary for landing an excellent TWC internship. The first step is to find out who is the Washington Center liaison on your campus. Start with your career resources office. If you can't determine who your liaison is, contact the Washington Center directly and they can guide you through the process. The website for TWC is: www.twc.edu.

TWC is a competitive situation and requires that all students apply to their program. Once you're accepted to one of TWC's programs, you are assigned to a member of the Internship Management Team, who will send your application to potential internship sites based on your interests and the needs of the sites. Internship sites that are a good fit will review your application materials in light of competition. TWC Internship sites compete against each other to attract the interns they most desire.

As the process moves along, a representative from a prospective internship location may contact you by phone and may want to set up a time for a phone interview. Like any interview for a job or an internship, you should spend some time developing a few questions you can ask the interviewer about the organization to show your interest and enthusiasm.

Our university has a great relationship with the Washington Center. Twice each year, the Washington Center representative visits our campus to discuss their excellent programs. Students meet representatives from TWC and our campus liaison and start the ball rolling.

Local Nonprofits

DON'T IGNORE LOCAL NONPROFITS. Many are eager to get some good interns on board. In our area (Southeastern Massachusetts), the Southcoast Hospital Group is the largest employer and they have shown great interest in getting our students in as interns. We also have relied on the New Bedford Whaling Museum, the New Bedford Museum of Glass, the Zeiterion Performing Arts Center, CEDC (Volunteer Income Tax Assistance program), the Fall River and New Bedford Chambers of Commerce as they have all utilized interns in the past.

Nonprofits usually don't pay interns although a small percentage of nonprofits do, usually at minimum wage rates. For example, at the University of Massachusetts Dartmouth, we received a Creative Economy Grant from the UMass President's Office to pay interns to work at the New Bedford Glass Museum. Therefore, sometimes there is money available through grants or donations to fund nonprofit internships, however, if you are interested in interning in the nonprofit world, your expectations should probably be that pay would not be involved.

Doing an internship for a nonprofit organization is quite different than working in a for profit organization. In a nonprofit, there are no stockholders and no one shares in the annual profits or losses. Instead there are stakeholders, entities that interact and sometimes benefit from the works of the nonprofit. Nonprofit organizations include charities, universities, government agencies, religious organizations, and some hospitals.

Nonprofit organizations can be robust economic engines. In their book: *Forces for Good, The Six Practices of High-Impact Nonprofits*, authors Leslie Crutchfield and Heather McLeod Grant, profile large nonprofits such as America's Second Harvest, City Year, Exploratorium, Habitat for Humanity, The Heritage Foundation, Self-Help and Teach for America – all large nonprofit corporations that need people in the areas of accounting, finance, MIS, and marketing.

Attending Job Fairs

ALTHOUGH 80% OR MORE OF THE activity at job fairs involves full-time job opportunities, sometimes company representatives collect résumés for internships. Find out when you school will be holding its job fairs. Most schools hold one in the fall and another in the spring. Also, see if there are job fairs held at other schools nearby. Bring copies of résumés and business cards. Approach the tables or kiosks of employers that interest you and simply state: "Are you hiring interns?[2]" I have taken this approach on behalf of students at my school and have uncovered many internship opportunities. Even if you get a "No" follow up with something like: "Well if you change your mind or if anyone else in your organization might want to bring on an intern, please keep me in mind." They may be willing to take your résumé and pass it along. You need to be constantly sowing seeds that may someday sprout into internships or job offers.

---

[2] Here's some advice from PWC on what to do at networking events and job fairs. "When you meet a recruiter or company representative, shake his or her hand confidently and make direct eye contact. Remember to listen as much (if not more) than you talk. Yes, you are promoting yourself, but you don't want to dominate the entire conversation. Request a business card from the recruiter or any professional contacts you meet so you can follow up after the event."

Job Shadowing

SOME CAREER DEVELOPMENT CENTERS at colleges and universities and some business colleges or departments set up job shadowing for undergraduate students. Job shadowing is a career exploration activity that gives students the opportunity to spend time with a professional currently working in a student's career field of interest. For example, an accounting student could spend a day on an audit with a CPA. Job shadowing offers a chance to see what it's like working in a specific job. Although job shadowing is not an internship, it could lead to an internship. If you are able to job shadow a professional and like what you see, be proactive and ask if there are internship opportunities with their company. Even if there are no current opportunities, something might come available in the future or your contact might know of a friend or colleague that would be willing to bring you on as an intern. Remember, you need to be constantly sowing seeds that may someday sprout into internships or job offers.

The alumni of your college are a good place to start when looking for a job shadow opportunity so you may want to visit your career development center and/or the alumni office of your school for possible job shadow leads. Sometimes business colleges have advisory boards made up of local business professionals and board members often volunteer their services for such assistance as job shadowing. Large organizations and government agencies also offer job-shadowing programs for students and if you are interested in a particular company, you may want to call their human resources office and inquire into the possibility of job shadowing. Check with organizations of interest to see if there is someone currently working in your career field of interest who would be interested in hosting a job shadow for one or more days over the course of the summer or during a winter break.

If you do job shadow someone, be sure to send a follow-up thank you note and if you are still interested in the company as a possible internship site, be sure to mention in your thank-you note that you would be interested in any internship opportunities that the company might have in your area of interest (accounting, finance, marketing, MIS, HR, etc.) You can also include a copy of your résumé with the thank you note.

Informational Interviewing

ANOTHER TECHNIQUE THAT COULD lead to an internship (or a full-time job) is informational interviewing. As primarily a fact finding mission, an informational interview is much less stressful than the usual interviewing situation and it is one of the few times when the interviewee leads the interview. It also allows you to showcase your poise, communication skills, knowledge of the company, and knowledge of the profession of your interest. Informational interviewing is a great technique for students looking for internships or permanent jobs. The key is to be very prepared when you start the interview and to have well-organized notes and questions to refer to. Here are some suggested questions that you could incorporate into an informational interview. Keep in mind that it should last no longer than 30 minutes so you don't want to ask all the questions on this list. Tailor the list below to meet your needs and discuss your list of questions with your career development advisor or academic advisor before going to the interview.

- What is your title and can you describe your job?

- Are there other commonly used titles for these positions?

- What is your typical day like?

- Is the work typically routine or does it vary significantly on a daily basis?

- What degrees or certification do people in your position seek?

- What type of experience is needed to do your job?

- What type of entry level position or internship would be a good stepping stone to your position?

- Does your organization offer internships or do you know other organizations that offer internships in the field?

- What are the key personal characteristics for success in this field?

- What opportunities for advancement exist?

- Can you describe the salary ranges of typical jobs within the company or field? (Don't ask the person how much they make–ask for a broad salary range or ask how you can find out what a typical salary range would be)

- Are hours set or is their flexibility in work times?

- What demands and frustrations typically accompany this type of work?

- What types of technology are used in this field?

- Would you offer any advice or suggestions for someone considering going into the field given what you know now?

- What are the satisfying and/or rewarding aspects of working in this field?

Be sure to follow up your informational interview with a thank you note.

Service Learning and Civic Engagement Projects

MANY COLLEGES AND UNIVERSITIES are encouraging and in some cases requiring that students complete service learning and other civic engagement projects. At the University of Massachusetts Dartmouth, we have the Leduc Center for Civic Engagement[3], which among other important responsibilities arranges service learning and other civic engagement projects with community partners. The Community Service Act of 1990, which authorized the Learn and Serve America grant program, defines service learning as:

---

[3] Here's how Civic Engagement and Service learning are defined at the Leduc Center for Civic Engagement at the University of Massachusetts Dartmouth: "*Civic engagement has been defined as actions constructed to identify and address issues of public concern. The University of Massachusetts Dartmouth, through the activities organized by the Leduc Center for Civic Engagement, aspires to meet the challenge of providing active student learning opportunities while meeting a community need. Service learning is a methodology that melds community service with classroom learning goals. Service learning augments the acquisition of skills and knowledge through experiential applications that meet the needs of a community and simultaneously fosters civic responsibility.*" (Source: UMASS Dartmouth website – http://www.umassd.edu/seppce/centers/cce/

> *a method under which students or participants learn and develop through active participation in thoughtfully organized service that is conducted in and meets the needs of a community; is coordinated with an elementary school, secondary school, institution of higher education, or community service program, and with the community; and helps foster civic responsibility; and that is integrated into and enhances the academic curriculum of the students, or the educational components of the community service program in which the participants are enrolled; and provides structured time for the students or participants to reflect on the service experience.*

Like internships, service-learning projects are part of experiential learning. Some of our students have been able to transform a service learning project or a short-term volunteer project into an internship. For example, we have accounting students who volunteer for about 50 hours during the spring semester preparing income tax returns for low-income families.

A local economic development agency coordinates that program and after seeing the fine work of our students has offered semester long internships that involve a variety of task in the operation of the office. Service learning and civic engagement projects may often lead to opportunities for you to showcase your talents and provide another interesting entry on your résumé´.

Entrepreneurship Forums and Incubators

AN OFTEN OVERLOOKED BUT VERY effective strategy when searching for an internship is face-to-face networking at entrepreneur forums and at local business incubators. For students who are looking to intern in entrepreneurial settings, I recommend attending entrepreneurship forums that are often periodically offered in cities and towns that are near universities and colleges.

Big schools like Harvard and Stanford have made entrepreneurial forums very popular,, but smaller schools like my school–UMass Dartmouth are associated with such events. We have a facility called the Advanced Technology & Manufacturing Center (ATMC) that is located a few miles from our campus.

The ATMC houses an active business incubator, a prototype lab and a conference center. About once a month, the ATMC hosts the Southern New England Entrepreneurs Forum (SNEEF). SNEEF is made up of a membership of local entrepreneurs and angel investors. The public is invited to their monthly meetings, which typically offer a speaker and a social hour.

Students have been successful at generating internship leads at these types of events. In addition, any incubator facility—a building that hosts and supports fledging start-up companies——often welcomes applications from students looking to do an internship. Each year, some of our business students intern at the ATMC and for some of the incubator companies at that facility.

Prepare a Cover Letter

IF YOU COME UP WITH SOME SOLID internship leads, send a letter and résumé showing your interest in landing an internship and follow-up with a phone call a few days later. The follow-up is very important. Don't hesitate to let the employer know that you are interested in interning at their company. Some of my students hesitate to follow-up but I insist that they make the call or send follow-up emails. An effective strategy is to show up at the employer and ask to talk to a human resources representative.

On the next page is a form letter that I give to our students to use in a search for an internship. I encourage them to customize this template to meet their specific needs. Points that you should incorporate into an internship inquiry cover letter include:

- Information about and perhaps a link to a webpage describing the internship program

- Your major and if you have a high GPA–your overall GPA and your GPA within your major

- Why the company or nonprofit is of interest to you

- A reference to your résumé

Your cover letter should be no more than one page and should be addressed to a specific individual–if possible. Stay away from demanding a certain pay level or hourly wage rate. Such a demand will find your letter and résumé in the waste basket. Be sure to include contact information near the end of the letter even if you have it on your résumé. Include your email and phone number.

If you don't hear from anyone from the organization within a week or two of sending the letter (wait a reasonable time period) then follow-up with a phone call. If your letter is in response to a specific internship position posting, simply ask if the position has been filled and if it hasn't ask if there are any questions you could answer about your résumé. If your letter is unsolicited, ask if there are any questions you could answer and if it might be possible to get an interview. Many prospective employers and internship providers like students who are proactive.

COVER LETTER

I am a (junior or senior) (accounting, finance, marketing, MIS, management) major at the Charlton College of Business, University of Massachusetts Dartmouth. My program allows me to earn three business elective credits by interning at a local company or agency. I am interested in developing an internship with your organization and have included my résumé for your review. [You should state why the particular organization is of interest to you.]

Internships-for-credit require a minimum of 9 hours per week for a total of 135 hours on the job along with the completion of an internship course. My internship will be monitored by a business professor and I will be required to complete several assignments, including a term paper, as part of my internship course.

You can learn more about the Charlton College of Business internship program by visiting:

www.umassd.edu/charlton/internship.cfm

I would also be happy to meet with you or another representative of your company to explore this possibility. I can be reached at (telephone number) or by email at (email address).

Sincerely,

Your name

Prepare a Solid Résumé

When students visit with me to talk about how to land an excellent internship, the first thing I always ask is if they have a résumé. Often I will ask the student to have the résumé´ reviewed by one of our career counselors. The résumé for an internship is really no different from the résumé for a permanent job. The format of a résumé is important but with résumé software and MS Word résumé templates, there is no reason to not have a perfect looking résumé. If you don't have a great looking résumé, I suggest you work with the career resource center of your school to generate one.

For the person conducting your interview for an internship, be sure your résumé communicates such things as special skills, employment history, other experiential activities such as volunteer work, service learning, prior internships, and community service. You should note on your résumé your participation in student-run clubs, professional associations, and collegiate sports.

Some students have told me that they don't want to put their part-time jobs such as waitressing, pumping gas, or working at a lumber yard on the résumé because they feel those are not professional experiences. I suggest that any part-time jobs that you have held for more than six months should be on the résumé. I have been told by many recruiters and executives that they like to see that and that the student has held part-time jobs—even the most menial and blue collar jobs—because those jobs show that a student can get work done.

PricewaterhouseCoopers LLP, the large international accounting firm, has what they call a PWC Brand Week–a series of workshops geared towards helping individuals develop their own personal brand[4]. Here's some advice from PWC Brand Week regarding résumés.

LIMIT YOUR BRILLIANCE TO ONE PAGE. Remember that your résumé is a marketing tool and not a laundry list of everything you've ever done. By keeping your résumé short, you're demonstrating that you can edit yourself and sell your skills clearly and concisely.

PROFESSIONALIZE YOUR CONTACT INFO. Résumés featuring email addresses like ILovePuppies@internetserviceprovider.com may not seem professional to the company to which you are applying. Make sure your email address and the voice mail messages on any phone numbers you list are 100 percent professional and appropriate.

INCLUDE UNPAID EXPERIENCE. Just because you didn't get compensated for certain work doesn't mean it shouldn't count as experience for your résumé. By all means include

---

[4] You can download a copy of the PWC personal brand experience workbook 2011 at www.pwc.com/us/en/careers/pwctv/2011/assets/personal-brand-experience-workbook.pdf

internships, volunteer work, and part-time jobs if you achieved significant results or learned important skills in those positions.

QUANTIFY YOUR RESULTS. Employers don't just want to know what you did; they also want to know what results you accomplished. How many people did you oversee as a store manager? How much money did you save as the junior class as treasurer? Quantifying your accomplishments demonstrates not only what you achieved, but also the fact that you track your results.

PRIORITIZE YOUR POINTS. When you list bullet points under each position or activity on your résumé, be sure to place the most important task, accomplishment, or responsibility first. Most readers of your résumé will pay close attention to what you've chosen to feature as the first item on each list.

CUSTOMIZE YOUR RÉSUMÉ FOR DIFFERENT OPPORTUNITIES. Employers can tell when they are seeing a generic résumé that is being blasted out to anyone and everyone. It's fine to have such a résumé as a template, but then you need to customize it for various opportunities by featuring the experience, keywords, and activities that best suit the requirements of that particular position.

INCLUDE ONLY INTERESTING INTERESTS. When it comes to listing interests or hobbies on your résumé, only mention something that is particularly unique, uncommon, or memorable. For example, "Founding president of first-ever Tae Kwon Do Club at my university" or "three-time finisher of Chicago Marathon." Generic interests such as "travel and reading" are nice, but they don't add much.

DELETE THE REFERENCE REFERENCES. Don't waste precious space on your résumé with "References available upon request." Potential employers will request a list of references if they want one.

NEVER LIE, EXAGGERATE, OR TWIST THE TRUTH. There are so many reasons not to lie on a résumé. First of all, if your lie or truth stretching gets discovered, you'll lose a job opportunity with that company forever. Second, if you exaggerate your skills, such as being fluent in French when you really just studied it in junior high, your lie will become extremely obvious the day you start your job and you lack the skills you said you had. You should certainly cast yourself in the most positive light, but never, ever take it too far.

PROOFREAD, AND THEN PROOFREAD AGAIN. Finally, there is absolutely, positively no excuse for a single typo or grammar mistake on a résumé. Once you've proofread your résumé and feel confident it's perfect, have at least two other people review it for mistakes, misspellings, and formatting glitches. You can never check your résumé too many times.

Source: PricewaterhouseCoopers LLP

About 95% of our (Charlton College of Business) internship job postings require that the student send a résumé as an attachment to an email. In that case, I advise students to also include a cover letter as an attachment. If the posting says do not include a cover letter you can use the email as a brief yet pseudo cover letter.

Prepare an Internship Proposal

ALL THE INTERNSHIP POSITIONS THAT I post on my blog[5] are approved internships. That means students who land those internships can take our internship course and receive three credits for a business elective, but often students find internships and need to submit them for my approval before they can enroll in our internship course. I must approve all internships-for-credit and I do that after performing some due diligence (homework).

Once you have found an internship, depending on the policies and procedures of your school, you

---

[5] My blog is: http://www.businessinternships.blogspot.com/

may need to present the internship to a sponsoring professor or your internship director for approval. Some schools require that you prepare an internship proposal that describes the job or project that you will be working on. The proposal must contain enough information for your professor or internship director to make a decision as to the learning possibilities of the opportunity. If you are required to prepare an internship proposal, be sure to include within your proposal all of the following (and please check to see if other information is required by your school):

- Description of the company including the mission, location, sales and market coverage. Please include your web URL (if you have it)
- Overview of the internship objectives
- Primary duties and responsibilities
- What you will learn from this experience
- Job title
- Compensation
- Skills required
- Hours of work
- Start and end dates
- Name of primary supervisor
- How you will be evaluated?

- Additional company contacts (if applicable)
- Name and title of the person providing this information (information should be gathered in collaboration with someone from the internship providing organization)

When deciding if I can approve an internship, I look for certain best practices. When searching and interviewing for an internship, students should also see evidence of best practices. Best practices by companies that bring on interns can take a variety of forms. Here are some of the common best practices:

THE PROVIDER INVESTS IN THE INTERN. A best practice is for the internship company or nonprofit to invest money and time in the intern. This means spending the time to provide a proper orientation and in some cases, paying the intern a good wage. Not all quality internships are paid ones and many nonprofits will not pay or are prohibited from paying, but many of the very best internships are paid. Examples include the big four accounting internships and UPS. Periodic workshops and formal training are other ways to invest in the intern. Our college has had students intern with Nestle Waters/Poland Springs which provides formal training, field trips, and days out on the delivery trucks as a way of educating the intern on operations.

THE INTERNSHIP PROVIDER SHOULD HAVE A JOB DESCRIPTION. A written job description that makes it clear what is expected of the intern. Skills, knowledge, and abilities needed for the internship along with a well-written description of responsibilities goes a long way to helping the intern become productive early on. A job description is a good first step in learning.

The internship should involve projects that connect to classroom learning. The best internships connect what the student has learned before the internship to the real world. Internships often present the test first and then the lesson. Accounting interns prepare tax returns or perform audits and then can reflect back on what was learned and how book knowledge plays out in the real world.

QUALITY INTERNSHIPS HAVE DOCUMENTED CHECKPOINTS AND FREQUENT FEEDBACK. The best internships are those monitored by someone–perhaps a faculty member or an intern manager at the firm. In our internship program (Charlton College of Business) we require that the students take an internship course with all aspects documented in an online-learning system. Students file weekly work journals, provide written job descriptions, take quizzes, and provide reflective writing assignments. The best CPA firm internships require weekly meetings with a supervisor and constant feedback. End-of-internship activities such as exit interviews and written evaluations also provide additional feedback and documented learning.

THE INTERNSHIP PROVIDER SHOULD CREATE A PROFESSIONAL WORK ENVIRONMENT. The company should provide an adequate work area for the intern. Such provisions–a desk, computer, telephone, office supplies etc.–increase the odds that the internship will be an excellent experience. Student interns need adequate resources to carry out their tasks.

THERE SHOULD BE OTHER VALUABLE INTANGIBLES EVIDENT IN A QUALITY INTERNSHIP. In addition to learning new technical skills and knowledge via an internship, the best internship experiences help the student learn to practice persistence, solve problems, exhibit a positive-attitude, become more productive, hone their people and networking skills, and to plan, and prioritize.

Internship Interview

AN INTERVIEW FOR AN INTERNSHIP IS similar to the interview for a permanent job. The first step: be very prepared. If you respond to an internship announcement or position posting, be sure to carefully read again before the interview and use it as your initial source to generate questions to ask at the appropriate time during the interview.

Show up at least 10 minutes before the interview and be appropriately dressed. If you are not sure what to wear, consult with a valued advisor like a career resource center professional, a knowledgeable friend or relative, a professor in your field, or your academic advisor. Being over dressed is better than underdressed at any job interview. In an interview, the way you are dressed plays an important supporting role. I have sat on many search and screen committees to hire faculty and staff at universities and colleges and the way people dress is definitely a factor. One piece of advice I recently heard is: do not wear what you wear to the clubs on Friday and Saturday evenings! Business dress is not the same as club dress. You need to dress more like a "preppy" than a "clubber".

Keep in mind that in many interviews, your conduct, your interpersonal skills and your ability to articulate intelligent and well thought out responses to questions are the most important elements. So don't overly stress about how you look but it is a consideration and you need to make good clothes choices, even for an interview as appropriate attire supports your image as a person who takes the interview process seriously and understands the nature of the company and industry in which you are trying to become employed.

For some internships such as those in marketing or store management, customer contact and image presented to the customer is critical. In such situations, your attire will be judged more critically. I tell students to be conservative. Your clothing should be noticed as being appropriate and well fitting, but it should not be flashy, revealing or take center stage. If you are primarily remembered for your interview attire, then you probably made an error in judgment.

One pitfall that students make is that because they are aware that employees of an organization dress casually on the job, they too dress casually for the interview and sometime that bothers the interviewer. Dress up for the interview unless you are specifically told otherwise by the employer.

Being a male, I am more comfortable advising the guys on what to wear to an interview. I suggest conservative dress—a navy, or gray suit or a navy, black, or gray sport jacket with conservatively contrasting dress slacks (gray, tan, black, or navy). Choose a solid or very subtle weave pattern or plaid (the kind that look solid across a room). Wool, wool blends, or very high quality natural and synthetic fiber blends are acceptable fabrics for a conservative men's suit. Stay away from polyester that looks like it was produced using a waffle iron and don't wear one of those leisure suits from the 1970s!

If you are unsure about mixing and matching a sport coat with pants, then go with a suit. A white or light blue dress shirt works well with a conservative (not bright or flashy) silk tie properly tied and contrasting in a color that is darker than the shirt. Your shoes should be dress shoes that are clean, polished, and coordinate with the slacks and your belt (please wear a belt!). The rule of thumb is that if you wear blue or gray slacks you should wear black dress shoes.

I find that most of our female students have a better fashion sense than the guys when it comes to dressing for an interview. Even in my own family, my daughters are the experts even when it comes to advising my sons on what to wear to an interview, and I am not as comfortable advising the ladies on how to dress. My only advice is that women also need to be conservative paying attention to conservative colors and cuts (blouses, skirts, and dresses).

I suggest that women who are unsure about what to wear to an internship interview do some Google searches on that topic. There are some very good webpages on college career resource sites with good interview attire advice. I especially like the Virginia Tech's site at:

www.career.vt.edu/interviewing/interviewappearance.html#say.

Getting to the interview site early and being properly dressed is all part of being prepared for the interview, but so is any research you can do on the organization[6]. Certainly your first step should be to review the content of the company's website. When I post an internship announcement I usually include the company's website address so our students can familiarize themselves with the history, mission, product and service offerings of the organization.

You should also Google the company to see what has been in the news recently about the firm. As you are doing your review of the company website, articles, and annual reports, write down any questions that might pop into your head. These might be good material for the interview

---

[6] Here is some advice from PWC.. Spend at least 30 to 60 minutes researching the organization whose event or interview you are attending so you can show why your skill set is a good fit. Review the organization's website to learn about its mission, lines of business, culture and entry-level positions. Do a general web search to review any recent news about the organization and the overall industry in which it operates. Ask members of your career center staff to tell you more about the organization and its history with your university.

when inevitably the interviewer will ask: "Do you have any questions for me?" Also, a common question that an internship interviewer will ask is: "What do you know about us?

To anticipate that question you can jot down the answers to some of these questions:

- How large is the company and when was it established?
- What products and services does it produce?
- What new products or services is the company currently offering or planning to offer?
- Where is the company located?
- What is the company's reputation?
- Who are the major competitors?

Students always ask me what types of questions they will be asked in an interview as if I have some type of inside track. There is no set standard for internship interview questions. Some students have told me of interviews where there seemed to be an immediate connection between the student and the interviewer and very few questions were asked.

Students have told me: "He did all the talking and asked me what questions I had and then offered me the internship." And although that type of interview can happen, it is the exception rather than the rule. You need to anticipate questions and be prepared.

Here's a list of possible internship interview questions:

- Can you tell me about yourself?
- What is your GPA overall and in your major?
- What have been your favorite business courses? Favorite non-business courses?
- What courses do you dislike?
- What do you know about our company?
- What skills and abilities will you bring to the internship?
- What types of part-time jobs have you had while in school?
- What have you learned from your part-time jobs and how will that help you in this internship?
- What kind of service learning projects, volunteer work or community service have you done while in school?
- Tell me about your dream job.
- Where do you see yourself working when you graduate?

- What extracurricular activities have you been involved in? Are you a member any student clubs or associations such as the Institute of Management Accountants, State Society of CPAs, American Marketing Association, American Management Association etc.?

- What books have you read recently?

- What are your strengths and weaknesses?

- What questions do you have for me?

- Will you get credit for doing this internship? How many credits?

- What will we have to do to help you earn credit on this internship?

There are many other questions that could be asked. The type of internship can influence the kinds of questions the interviewer will ask. For example, the internship (such as an auditing one) may require that you need a car to travel to client sites[7].

---

[7] For example, an interviewer from a CPA firm might also ask you about your plans for graduate school (because of the 150 credit requirement in most states for CPAs), your plan to take the CPA exam, any other firms local, regional or national you are considering, if you have a vehicle, your class schedule to see if it could mess with audit schedules, if you prefer to work as part of a group or individually and why, and what is your problem solving approach when faced with a difficult challenge/problem? (Source: Mr. Steven Loffredo, Director of Human Resources for KLR, a regional CPA firm in

In preparation for your interview, practice your responses–first by writing them down and then verbally. It would be best if you could do a mock interview with a friend or with an advisor before your internship interview.

Another part of being prepared for the internship interview is assembling the right materials. Make sure you bring all the proper materials such as:

CURRENT COPIES OF YOUR RÉSUMÉ - bring a few copies even if you know the interviewer has a copy. They may forget their copy or they may bring another person to the interview who should also receive a copy. At a minimum, having copies with you makes you feel prepared and you can keep it in front of you as the interview is being conducted to serve as a reference.

LIST OF REFERENCES - have three or four names of former supervisors and professors on one sheet of paper and be ready to offer the list if asked. Be sure you have gotten permission to give these references from the people on your list.

TRANSCRIPTS - some internship providers want a copy of the student's transcripts at the interview. To be safe, have a copy ready to give.

NOTEBOOK - have a pad of paper or a notebook that you can take notes in. It is fine to

---

Providence, RI.)

write your own questions in the notebook, but don't become pre-occupied with the notebook or with taking notes. A quick notation once in a while is fine and shows you are organized and like to document important thoughts, but don't be writing frequently and don't record direct quotes from the interviewer. It is also proper to ask if it is fine to take a few notes, but even after getting permission, be conservative on the amount of note taking you do.

These materials should be in a folder or a case and easily accessible to you at the start of your interview.

Finally, have a set of questions ready to ask the interviewer. Here are some possibilities:

- What is the start date of this internship? End date?

- Where will I be working and what is the office environment like?

- Who will be my supervisor/mentor and what is that person's background?

- Will I receive frequent feedback from my supervisor/mentor so I can learn a great deal and be a contributor?

- Is there a written job description for this internship position?

- Are there other interns that I will be working with?

- Are there transportation or travel requirements?

- Is this paid or unpaid? If it is paid, do you have an idea of what the hourly rate is?

- How many hours per week?

- Is there an orientation period or will I be expected to start right in on my duties?

- What will the training be like? Is it all on the job? Is it a combination of on the job and formal training?

- What are the company's customers like?

- Is there any chance that the internship could be a full-time position at some point?

Internship Resources

THERE ARE A NUMBER OF BOOKS AND web resources that might be of value to a college student searching for a great business internship. Unfortunately, these publications usually cover all types of internships and don't provide a focus on business internships. They also rarely provide information on local smaller companies and nonprofits that are looking for internships so my advice to students is to utilize these publications, but also use other strategies for landing a great internship.

Vault Guide to Top Internships

By Rebecca Rose, Samer Madeh, Mark Oldman and the staff of Vault

This guide is published annually by Vault Inc. and is available through bookstores and Amazon.com. It profiles hundreds of internships and includes an annual top ten list of the best internships in America, however, the guide offers no explanation as to how the ranking is determined and many of their top internships are not business oriented. The 2011 edition of the book ranked the top ten internships as follows alphabetical order:

- Boston Consulting Group
- Capital Fellows Programs
- Deloitte LLP
- Garmin International
- Google, Inc.
- J.P. Morgan's Investment Bank
- NASA
- Nickelodeon Animation Studios
- Northwestern Mutual Financial Network
- Smithsonian Institution

Vault also ranks the top finance internships. Here they are for 2011:

- AT&T Financial Leadership Program
- Blackstone Group
- Credit Suisse Group
- Deutsche Bank
- Goldman Sachs and Company
- J.P. Morgan's Investment Bank
- Lazard
- Morgan Stanley
- Northwestern Mutual Financial Network
- UBS Investment Bank

Source: www.vault.com

Accounting Internships

Accounting firms have a long history with internships and most firms do a quality job managing interns and helping them learn. Below are the addresses of the large accounting firms, all of which have outstanding and very competitive internship programs. In addition, many regional and local firms hire interns–especially during tax season.

DELOITTE & TOUCHE

National Campus Recruiting

Ten Westport Road

P.O. Box 820

Wilton, CT 06897-0820

Tel: (203) 761-3000 Fax: (203) 563-2324

Website: www.deloitte.com/careers

Deloitte & Touche offers internship opportunities to qualified students in offices around the country. Internships are offered in the spring (January-March) and summer (June-August) and are open to students from colleges and universities and who have strong academic credentials. Participants get on-the-job training as well as technical and business-oriented education in the classroom. Interns are hired in all functions of the firm: Assurance, Financial Advisory Services (FAS), Enterprise Risk Services (ERS), Human Capital, Solutions, or Tax Services.

ERNST & YOUNG LLP

National Director of Campus Recruiting

1285 Avenue of the Americas

New York, NY 10019

Tel: (212) 773-3000

Website: www.ey.com

Ernst & Young LLP sponsors and participates in INROADs, a career development program for talented minorities in business and industry. Internships are offered to students who participate in INROADS in Ernst & Young offices around the country. Additionally, the firm offers internships in the summer and spring semesters to students from selected colleges and universities.

KPMG LLP

University Relations

Three Chestnut Ridge Road

Montvale, NJ 07645-0435

Tel: (201) 307-7000 Fax: (201) 307-7575

Website: www.kpmgcampus.com

KPMG views its internship program as a "stepping stone" for a career at KPMG, all of the programs and processes it uses over the course of the internship are similar to those it uses for full-time professionals. Training exposes interns to the KPMG culture and leadership, and provides a knowledge base to draw upon throughout the remainder of the internship. After training, interns are assigned to a variety of engagements. KPMG has two internship programs.

Winter/Spring - this program begins with training the first week of January and is a one to three month program.

Summer - this program begins with training in June and is a seven to ten week program.

PRICEWATERHOUSECOOPERS

Recruiting

1301 Avenue of the Americas

New York, NY 10019

Tel: (646) 394-1000

Website: www.pwc.com/uscareers

MCGLADREY LLP

The fifth largest U.S. provider of assurance, tax and consulting services, with nearly 6,500 professionals and associates in more than 70 offices nationwide. McGladrey has two defined internship periods, which should accommodate most university student's schedules:

Winter internships – January through March/April

Summer internships – June through August

Website: mcgladrey.com

CBIZ AND MAYER HOFFMAN MCCANN

Website: www.cbiz.com/careers/

GRANT THORNTON

Website: www.GrantThornton.com/CampusCareers

Collegegrad.com

Collegegrad.com is a website that helps college graduates search for job openings. As part of their service, they rank the best internships. Visit their website to see the current list of "best internships." According to the Collegegrad.com website, they rank internships based on how "dedicated [the company is] to the training and development of talent through internships."

Idealist.org

Idealist is a website that lists internships with nonprofits nationwide. There are thousands of internship postings on Indealist.com and almost all are unpaid, as is typical with nonprofits. Many of these internships offer very rewarding experiences and insights into nonprofit management, fundraising, communication, operations, sales, and marketing. Visit www.idealist.org for more details.

What Color is Your Parachute?

A book that I first read over 25 years ago and is still relevant today when you are trying to find a suitable career path is What Color is Your Parachute?: A Practical Manual for Job-Hunters and Career-Changers. It us written by Richard N. Bolles and is a classic. It sits on my bookcase in my office and I refer to it often. Make it part of your career development library. It has great suggestions such as how to use informational interviewing to land you a great internship and possibly a permanent job that matches with your aptitudes.

Businessweek

Bloomberg Businessweek publishes an annual list of the Best Internships and ranks the leading programs according to data such as pay and the percentage of interns who get full-time jobs. To compile the 2009 list, Businessweek judged employers based on survey data from 60 career services directors around the country and a separate survey completed by each employer. They also consider how each employer fared in the annual Best Places to Launch a Career ranking of top U.S. entry-level employers released in

September of 2009 by Businessweek. The top ten programs of the 2009 list were follows:

1. Deloitte
2. KPMG
3. Ernst and Young
4. Proctor and Gamble
5. PriceWaterhouseCoopers
6. Goldman Sachs
7. Target
8. UBS
9. Accenture
10. General Electric

Indeed.com

Indeed.com is a search engine for jobs, allowing job seekers to find jobs posted on thousands of company career sites and job boards. One very useful feature of Indeed.com and one that I use and recommend to students is the ability to construct email alerts based on searches. Therefore, if you were looking for an internship in Boston, you can have Indeed.com send you daily email alerts showing internship postings by Boston-area employers.

Many of my students at the Charlton College of Business, University of Massachusetts Dartmouth, have found internships via Indeed.com and the daily email alerts that I receive from this service have helped me target good opportunities for our business majors.

I use key-word searches that combine functional areas of business such as accounting, finance, MIS, or marketing with geographical preferences (Boston, Springfield, Providence, RI, etc.) I suggest to students that they try several combinations of key-word searches for a few days to see what kind of yield they get and when they are satisfied with the e-harvest of internship postings, set the email alert feature.

Simply Hired

Simply Hired is also a search engine for jobs and like Indeed.com, it scours the Internet looking for jobs that match keywords and other folders that you can set up. Although I use both Indeed.com and Simplyhired.com to find internship postings that I pass along to our students, there is a great deal of overlap between the search results of both services. However, very often I do find unique results and by uncovering just a few new opportunities each week I feel my efforts are well spent.

Experience.com

Founded by Jennifer Floren, who had a vision of a better way for college students to prepare career paths and hunt for jobs, Experience is the leading provider of career services for students and alumni. Over three million students and alumni use Experience to find unique jobs and over 100,000 employers and alumni post job and internship opportunities at experience.com.

Check with your Career resource center or placement office to see if your school subscribes to Experience.com. Recently (Spring 2012), Experience.com has partnered with the Commonwealth of Massachusetts and set up a new portal called Mass Stay Here to help students learn about internship opportunities in the state of Massachusetts: (ma.experience.com/experience/login)

Internships.com

This portal claims to be the "world's largest internship marketplace." On one of my visits to the site, Internships.com stated that it had 40,667 internship positions from 12,700 companies located in 1,616 cities across all 50 states. For $20 per year, a student can get a premium subscription that includes such services as a résumé review and an "iCertified badge" for your Internships.com profile; a type of internship certification as a result of completing an online workshop on what is expected of interns. According to Internships.com, such a certification is attractive to prospective employers.

Blogs and Tweets

If you are not a student at the University of Massachusetts Dartmouth or a college or university nearby, my blogs and tweets will probably not help you land a specific internship. Most of the opportunities I describe in my blog entries or the daily tweets I send out are located within a 50 mile radius of North Dartmouth, Massachusetts. However, you are welcome to visit my blogs or follow me on @bizinternship (Twitter). I maintain two blogs that disseminate information on internships.

One of the blogs[8] provides mostly postings of current open internship positions that have come to my attention either through direct contact or from my web searches.

A second blog, www.internshipyak.blogspot.com, provides information, tips, and advice on how to land a business internship (college). I also post positive experiences of interns just as they have completed their assignments. By reading those comments, other students learn about good

---

[8] http://www.businessinternships.blogspot.com/

opportunities, the possible benefits of landing a great internship, and sticking it out to a final positive conclusion.

Checklist: Finding a Good Internship

- Search for internships using college resources such as Career Development Centers and online data bases of internship postings such as Experience.com and Internships.com.

- Search for internships on such services as Indeed.com and Simplyhired.com and set up email alerts so you can be notified when internships matching your keyword searches hit the web.

- Prepare a résumé and cover letter and drop them off at the human resources department at local businesses that interest you. Follow up in a few days with a phone call.

- Let your business professors, your parents, and your parents' colleagues, friends, and neighbors know that you are looking for an internship. They know people in the industry who may be looking for an intern.

- Talk to other students who have completed internships. Your peers are a great source of information regarding internships.

- Attend forums, college club meetings, and other events where you can network and meet people.

- Meet alumni, job shadow, conduct informational interviews and find other ways to get out of your comfort zone and make things happen.

- Build your own database or mailing list of possible internship providers and be ready to sell yourself by mailing out a well-written cover letter and résumé. Think about having business cards made to hand out at job fairs and other events that business people and nonprofit leaders might attend.

- Examine the possibilities of interning at a nonprofit or a government agency and if you complete a service learning project or are involved in other forms of civic engagement determine if your experience could be morphed into an internship.

- Attend college-sponsored events that attract alumni and be ready to introduce yourself and inquire about internship opportunities.

- Understand the best practices of quality internship providers and look for those practices in the internship position postings, job descriptions, and interviews.

- Be prepared for the internship interview and dress appropriately.

About the Author

MICHAEL P. GRIFFIN is a graduate of Providence College (BS 1980) and Bryant University (formerly Bryant College) (MBA 1982). He is also the Internship Director for the college. Mr. Griffin has worked for a number of employers including Fleet National Bank, E.F. Hutton and Company, and the Federal Home Loan Bank of Boston. Joining the University of Massachusetts Dartmouth in 1986, Mike served as Assistant to the Dean in the College of Business and Industry while teaching in the Accounting and Finance department. He has also taught in the Marketing/Business Information Systems department for five years and served as Assistant Dean for two years. His current course load includes Principles of Accounting, Cost Accounting, and the Internship course.

He is a Certified Management Accountant (CMA) and a Certified Financial Manager (CFM); the Institute of Management Accountants awards both designations. In addition, Michael holds the Chartered Financial Consultant (ChFC) designation from the American College and is a member of the Association of Certified Fraud Examiners.

Mr. Griffin is the author of many business books and has developed several software packages both for commercial and academic use. His latest book, MBA Fundamentals: Accounting and Finance was published by Kaplan Publishing. His latest educational tools are study sheets published by BarCharts Publishing Inc. (Accounting 2, Cost Accounting, Accounting Formulas and Equations) and Kaplan Publishing (Accounting Basics). His articles on such topics as internships, small business, and proposal writing have been published in such periodicals as Strategic Finance, The Accountant, International Journal of Enterprise Information Systems, and International Journal of Production Research. He has been a content consultant to a number of textbook publishers, including McGraw-Hill, Irwin, Addison Wesley, Pearson Education and Prentice Hall and has developed software for many software publishers including KMT Software Inc. Corel, Canon and Templatezone.com.

Michael is a past recipient of the Thomas J. Higgins Award for Excellence in Teaching, the 2011 Provost Best Practices Innovative Use of Technology Award, and the Walter Cass Faculty Recognition Award.

Acknowledgement

This book was edited by Ms. Kate Griffin, an English major at the University of North Carolina at Chapel Hill.

Internship Book

I have written a book called Business Internships. This book can be used as a basic internship course book or as a how to manual for anyone wanting to setup a successful internship experience. Whether you are looking to land a great internship or already have an internship and want to increase the odds that it will be an excellent learning experience, this book can help It is available at: www.lulu.com, search on Business internships. The ISBN is 978-1-4357-9016-2, copyright 2011, Michael P. Griffin.

HOW TO LAND AN EXCELLENT BUSINESS INTERNSHIP © 2012 Michael P. Griffin. All rights reserved.

Mr. Griffin can be reached at 508.910.6947 or by email: mgriffin@umassd.edu. Griffin maintains an internship which provides listings of current internship postings of interest to UMASS Dartmouth students. You can view the business internship blog at:

www.businessinternships.blogspot.com. The book, **BUSINESS INTERNSHIPS** by Michael P. Griffin can be ordered by visiting Lulu.com or by contacting Professor Griffin directly.

www.ingramcontent.com/pod-product-compliance
Lightning Source LLC
Chambersburg PA
CBHW070427180526
45158CB00017B/911